How Sweet The Name Of Jesus Sounds

TEN REFLECTIONS
AND MEDITATIONS
BASED ON
WORDS FROM
JOHN NEWTON'S
BELOVED HYMN

JAMES CAMPBELL

Ark House Press
arkhousepress.com

Ark House Press
arkhousepress.com

Cataloguing in Publication Data:
Title: How Sweet The Name Of Jesus Sounds
ISBN: 978-1-7635572-1-5 (pbk)
Subjects: REL055020   RELIGION / Christian Rituals & Practice / Worship & Liturgy; MUS009000 MUSIC / Religious / Contemporary Christian; MUS021000 MUSIC / Religious / Hymns

Design by initiateagency.com

HOW SWEET THE NAME OF JESUS SOUNDS

How sweet the name of Jesus sounds
in a believer's ear!
It soothes our sorrows, heals our wounds,
and drives away our fear.

It makes the wounded spirit whole
and calms the troubled breast,
is manna to the hungry soul
and to the weary, rest.

Dear name! the rock on which I build,
my shield and hiding place,
my never-failing treasury, filled
with boundless stores of grace.

Jesus, my shepherd, brother, friend,
my prophet, priest, and king,
my Lord, my life, my way, my end,
accept the praise I bring.

Weak is the effort of my heart,
And cold my warmest thought;
but when I see you as you are
I'll praise you as I ought.

Till then I would your love proclaim
with every fleeting breath,
and may the music of your name
refresh my soul in death.

John Newton

Contents

Preface

I love singing hymns. The words of the great hymn writers capture the truths of the gospel with simple clarity. And, importantly, the words are accompanied by music that imprints the words on our heart and mind and makes it easy to recall hymns and enjoy them at any time and place: in the proverbial shower, around the house, in the car, on a walk. You don't have to sing out loud (in my case just as well), but just let the tune and the words flow in your head. For me, after the Bible and the Anglican prayer book, the hymns of the great hymn writers powerfully portray the truths of the gospel.

But singing hymns has its dangers. Sometimes you can get caught up in the beauty of the music, the familiarity of the words, the encouragement of a congregation in full voice, an inspiring setting, and you can sing over truths the hymn writer is imparting. Sometimes it is only for a moment, but it could be the whole hymn.

A few Sundays ago this happened to me. As I sat down after singing one of my favourite hymns, I realised that I had just sung through one of the verses, without processing the depth of its message. When I got home I revisited this verse and realised that the words contained such a depth of meaning that I had not had time in the few seconds it took to sing the verse to process its contents.

This little book seeks to not only do this verse justice, but to demonstrate what a wonderful and complete Saviour we have in Jesus.

It is no secret that I am referring to John Newton's beautiful hymn *"How Sweet the Name of Jesus Sounds"*.

Introduction

John Newton wrote over three hundred hymns, an impressive output. Among his best known and most loved are, *"Amazing Grace"*, *"Glorious Things of Thee Are Spoken"*, *"How Sweet the Name of Jesus Sounds"*, and *"O for a Closer Walk with God"*. The full text of *"How Sweet the Name of Jesus Sounds"* is printed at the front of this little book.

In *"How Sweet the Name of Jesus Sounds"* the first two verses encourage believers to rely on Jesus when we are in dark places, or under stress either from secular pressure, our own weaknesses, or the devil's wiles. Perhaps the writer has in mind Jesus' words:

> *"Come to me, all you who are weary and burdened, and I will give you rest. Take my yoke upon you and learn from me, for I am gentle and humble in heart, and you will find rest for your souls. For my yoke is easy and my burden is light."* (Matthew 11:28-30)

In the third verse the hymn writer encourages us to build our lives around Jesus, our rock. Perhaps he has in mind the parable of the two builders.

"Therefore everyone who hears these words of mine and puts them into practice is like a wise man who built his house on the rock. The rain came down, the streams rose, and the winds blew and beat against that house; yet it did not fall, because it had its foundation on the rock. But everyone who hears these words of mine and does not put them into practice is like a foolish man who built his house on sand. The rain came down, the streams rose, and the winds blew and beat against that house, and it fell with a great crash." (Matthew 7:24-27)

Or perhaps he had in mind the supernatural sustenance of Jesus, the spiritual rock, when Paul speaks of the Israelites in 1 Corinthians 10:3-4:

"They all ate the same spiritual food and drank the same spiritual drink; for they drank from the spiritual rock that accompanied them, and that rock was Christ." (1 Corinthians 10:3-4)

The final two verses are an amalgamation of praise and a commitment to follow Jesus. The praise perhaps drawing on verses from Revelation:

"After this I looked, and there before me was a great multitude that no one could count, from every nation, tribe, people and language, standing before the throne and before the Lamb. They were wearing white robes and were holding palm branches in their hands. And they cried out in a loud voice:

"Salvation belongs to our God, who sits on the throne, and to the Lamb."

All the angels were standing around the throne and around the elders and the four living creatures. They fell down on their faces before the throne and worshiped God, saying:

"Amen! Praise and glory and wisdom and thanks and honor and power and strength be to our God for ever and ever. Amen!" (Revelation 7:9-12)

The commitment perhaps bearing in mind the Great Commission (Matthew 28:16-20), or he could have been thinking of Jesus' words to those who would follow him.

"Then he called the crowd to him along with his disciples and said: "Whoever wants to be my disciple must deny themselves and take up their cross and follow me. For whoever wants to save their life will lose it, but whoever loses their life for me and for the gospel will save it. What good is it for someone to gain the whole world, yet forfeit their soul? Or what can anyone give in exchange for their soul? If anyone is ashamed of me and my words in this adulterous and sinful generation, the Son of Man will be ashamed of them when he comes in his Father's glory with the holy angels." (Mark 8:34-38)

But now to the fourth verse, the verse that I had sung, but not had the time to process the depth of the words:

"Jesus, my shepherd, brother, friend, my prophet, priest, and king, my Lord, my life, my way, my end, accept the praise I bring."

In this remarkable verse, the writer lists ten cherished attributes of Jesus that he covets using the possessive 'my'. I am sure he thought deeply before penning these words. And, while it is appropriate for John Newton to make these declarations for himself, it is another matter for me to take his words and sing them, without thinking through the meaning of what I am singing. And as I said, I cannot do that in the time it takes to sing the verse.

The remainder of this little book are the joys I have found in reflecting and meditating on this verse. As this book is about a hymn, I have included a hymn that seems appropriate with each meditation.

My Shepherd

'The King of love my shepherd is'

Like me you probably don't know any real-life shepherds. But it is not too difficult from what we know to paint a picture of what we would expect a shepherd to look like.

I imagine a rugged, strong figure with a staff in his hand, standing at the gate of a brick or timber sheep-pen, as the early light of dawn is breaking. He opens the gate and calls out the sheep by name because he knows each one intimately. The shepherd leads off and the flock follow as he searches for areas where the pastures are fresh and green, and the streams are clear and clean. He takes special care of those of the flock who are in labour and the new lambs in season, as he knows they sustain and grow the flock.

At all times he cares for each member of the flock and is on the lookout for predators that may be prowling around, or thieves who may snatch outlying members of the flock, and he bravely fights off any who would do harm. Sometimes, if one of the flock goes astray, he searches for it and only returns when it has been safely recovered. He takes great care of the flock because they are his, or his family's, greatest asset.

Does Jesus look like this to you? Moses and David, the two great leaders of Israel thought so: they saw God as their shepherd.

At the end of his life, whilst blessing Joseph and his children, Moses said, *"God has been my shepherd all my life to this day"* (Genesis 48:15-16). And Moses would have been only too aware of the care with which God had led and protected him: saved from death in the Nile; banished from his homeland; chosen by God to be his emissary to Pharaoh and leader of the Israelites; leading a reluctant and rebellious bunch of 600,000 plus people for over forty years in a desert to the border of the Promised Land; prevented from entering the Promised Land because of his earlier rebellion against God.

David was no different, experiencing a lifetime of danger and challenge: having the responsibility of the family flock at an early age; standing up to and defeating the Philistine giant Goliath; being relentlessly pursued to death by Saul; chosen by God to be king of Israel; suffering public disgrace at God's hand for his adultery with Bathsheba; being pursued to death by his family and members of his army. But, like Moses, David always knew that he was in the providential care of a great shepherd. In one of his beautiful psalms David wrote, *"The Lord is my shepherd, I lack nothing."* (Psalm 23:1)

These two outstanding leaders of God's people faced great challenges and tribulation in their lives. The paths they walked over were often rocky, but they knew that they were under the hand of a shepherd whose only care was their eternal wellbeing.

The prophets, when speaking of the coming Messiah, prophesised that he would be the shepherd of God's people, Israel.

> *"He tends his flock like a shepherd:*
> *He gathers the lambs in his arms*

and carries them close to his heart;
he gently leads those that have young." (Isaiah 40:11)

"Hear the word of the Lord, you nations;
proclaim it in distant coastlands:
'He who scattered Israel will gather them
and will watch over his flock like a shepherd." (Jeremiah 31:10)

"For this is what the Sovereign Lord says: I myself will
search for my sheep and look after them. As a shepherd
looks after his scattered flock when he is with them, so
will I look after my sheep". (Ezekiel 34:11-12)

And, during his ministry Jesus clearly identified himself as Israel's shepherd.

"I am the good shepherd; I know my sheep and my sheep
know me— just as the Father knows me and I know the
Father—and I lay down my life for the sheep. I have
other sheep that are not of this sheep pen. I must bring
them also. They too will listen to my voice, and there shall
be one flock and one shepherd." (John 10:14-16)

Jesus adorned himself with the shepherd's role, spoken of by the prophets (John 10:1-18) and proved through God's actions time and again to Moses and David and many other Old Testament figures. He not only assumes the role, but emphasises that he is the 'good shepherd' who goes to the point of death for the flock.

Sheep tend to wander, and they can get lost momentarily behind some trees or rocks. But other times they may wander far away. Just like sheep, it can be easy for us to wander away from Jesus. The wonderful assurance the believer has is that Jesus has guaranteed that he will always be there to rescue his wayward sheep.

> *"And this is the will of him who sent me, that I shall lose none of all those he has given me, but raise them up at the last day. For my Father's will is that everyone who looks to the Son and believes in him shall have eternal life, and I will raise them up at the last day."* (John 6:39-40)

If you are like me, you need such a shepherd to watch over you, care about you, and gently guide you through your life. Sheep are dependant creatures: they don't know where the best grass and water is; they can wander into dangerous physical situations, and they are always at the mercy of predators and thieves. We are no different: we live in a dangerous world physically, emotionally, and spiritually. God gives us the choice: we can 'go it alone' or place ourselves in the hands of the 'good shepherd'.

Of course, we need to listen out for our shepherd's voice and heed his directions by reading his word and spending time with him in prayer. But how comforting it is to know that whatever our circumstances may be, rich or poor, in health or illness, stressed or at ease, on a spiritual high or in the valley of despair, like Moses and David, like John Newton, and millions of believers before us, when Jesus is our shepherd, you and I lack nothing.

MEDITATION – MY SHEPHERD

- Read (not sing!) through the words of the following hymn. Identify how the writer captures the truths of the gospel.

- Does the description of the shepherd in the reflection look right to you? What would you change? Add?

- What other Old Testament figures looked to the Lord as their shepherd? Examples?

- Have you been conscious of Jesus acting as your shepherd in your life? When? How?

- How do you keep in touch with your shepherd, Jesus?

- What are some of the things that can cause Jesus' sheep to be scattered or wander today?

- Use the link or code to listen to the choir sing the hymn and thank God that Jesus is your shepherd.

https://open.spotify.com/track/6XoKl8DlnSBek0kD5Q9UEQ?si=c4e327e2dd4f4195

THE KING OF LOVE MY SHEPHERD IS

The king of love my shepherd is,
whose goodness faileth never;
I nothing lack if I am his
and he is mine forever.

Where streams of living water flow
my ransomed soul he leadeth,
and where the verdant pastures grow
with food celestial feedeth.

Perverse and foolish oft I strayed,
but yet in love he sought me,
and on his shoulder gently laid,
and home rejoicing brought me.

In death's dark vale I fear no ill
with thee, dear Lord beside me;
thy rod and staff my comfort still,
thy cross before to guide me.

Thou spread'st a table in my sight;
thy unction grace bestoweth;
and O what transport of delight
from thy pure chalice floweth!

And so through all the length of days
thy goodness faileth never:
good Shepherd, may I sing thy praise
within thy house forever.

Henry Williams Baker

My Brother

'Breathe On Me Breath Of God'

I am an only child and sometimes I wonder what it would be like to have siblings. As I watch my four children and other families, I do feel I have missed out in some ways and may even be a little envious. So, when years ago I first read about the following event in Jesus' ministry, I was taken aback.

Matthew's record tells that once when Jesus was teaching the people, his mother and brothers arrived and wanted to speak to him. At first reading, Jesus' response seems a little surprising.

> *"While Jesus was still talking to the crowd, his mother and brothers stood outside, wanting to speak to him. Someone told him, "Your mother and brothers are standing outside, wanting to speak to you."*
>
> *He replied to him, "Who is my mother, and who are my brothers?" Pointing to his disciples, he said, "Here are my mother and my brothers. For whoever does the will of my Father in heaven is my brother and sister and mother."* (Matthew 12:46-50)

But, Jesus was not trying to diminish his earthly family or to fashion a new colloquial form of greeting. He wanted to make people realise that his eternal, heavenly family was made up of those who did the will of his Father, and they are his primary focus. But what is the will of Jesus' Father?

Once, after Jesus had miraculously fed five thousand people, he explained his role and the will of the Father.

> *"For I have come down from heaven not to do my will but to do the will of him who sent me. And this is the will of him who sent me, that I shall lose none of all those he has given me, but raise them up at the last day. For my Father's will is that everyone who looks to the Son and believes in him shall have eternal life, and I will raise them up at the last day."* (John 6:38-40)

If we look to Jesus and believe in him, the Father will grant us eternal life and Jesus will protect us, like a shepherd, and will keep us safe on the day of judgement. But there is more for those who look to Jesus as is explained in the introduction to John's gospel.

> *"In the beginning was the Word, and the Word was with God, and the Word was God. He was with God in the beginning. Through him all things were made; without him nothing was made that has been made. In him was life, and that life was the light of all mankind. The light shines in the darkness, and the darkness has not overcome it.*
>
> *There was a man sent from God whose name was John. He came as a witness to testify concerning that*

light, so that through him all might believe. He himself was not the light; he came only as a witness to the light.

The true light that gives light to everyone was coming into the world. He was in the world, and though the world was made through him, the world did not recognize him. He came to that which was his own, but his own did not receive him. Yet to all who did receive him, to those who believed in his name, he gave the right to become children of God— children born not of natural descent, nor of human decision or a husband's will, but born of God.

The Word became flesh and made his dwelling among us. We have seen his glory, the glory of the one and only Son, who came from the Father, full of grace and truth."
(John 1:1-14)

God tells us that we can be assured through our belief and faith in Jesus; that he counts us as his children and in a spiritual, familial sense, we share the same relationship with the Father as Jesus. What a wonderful blessing to have Jesus call us 'my brother' or 'my sister' and to be able to call Jesus 'my brother'. But this is much more than simply a nominal relationship; it is the foundation of God's new covenant that was promised in the prophets.

When Jesus was praying to his Father just before his arrest, he prayed first for the disciples, but then he prayed for all who would believe in him through their message.

"My prayer is not for them alone. I pray also for those who will believe in me through their message, that all of them may be one, Father, just as you are in me and I

am in you. May they also be in us so that the world may believe that you have sent me. I have given them the glory that you gave me, that they may be one as we are one—I in them and you in me—so that they may be brought to complete unity. Then the world will know that you sent me and have loved them even as you have loved me."
(John 17:20-23)

This is amazing, mystical, spiritual language. Jesus is in the Father and the Father is in Jesus and we sinners are lovingly included in this mystical communion. In essence, we who believe and do the will of the Father appear to have the same personal relationship that binds the Father and the Son! How can this be?

In the prophet Jeremiah we find the answer, as God lays out the new relationship or covenant between himself and mankind.

"The days are coming," declares the Lord, "when I will make a new covenant with the people of Israel and with the people of Judah. It will not be like the covenant I made with their ancestors when I took them by the hand to lead them out of Egypt, because they broke my covenant, though I was a husband to them," declares the Lord.

"This is the covenant I will make with the people of Israel after that time," declares the Lord. "I will put my law in their minds and write it on their hearts. I will be their God, and they will be my people. No longer will they teach their neighbor, or say to one another, 'Know the Lord,' because they will all know me, from the least

of them to the greatest," declares the Lord. "For I will
forgive their wickedness and will remember their sins no
more." (Jeremiah 31:31-34)

Through the prophet God tells us what he is going to do and,
hundreds of years later, Jesus explains to the disciples that this will
happen when the Father gives the Spirit of truth to those who believe.

"If you love me, keep my commands. And I will ask the
Father, and he will give you another advocate to help you
and be with you forever— the Spirit of truth. The world
cannot accept him, because it neither sees him nor knows
him. But you know him, for he lives with you and will
be in you. I will not leave you as orphans; I will come to
you. Before long, the world will not see me anymore, but
you will see me. Because I live, you also will live. On that
day you will realize that I am in my Father, and you are
in me, and I am in you. Whoever has my commands and
keeps them is the one who loves me. The one who loves me
will be loved by my Father, and I too will love them and
show myself to them." (John 14:15-21)

With this momentous shift, the mystical communion between
the Father, Jesus and all believers is complete and, with God's law in
our minds and written on our hearts, we will 'know the LORD' not
just as an abstract fact, but in the fullest way we can know a person.
And, the Holy Spirit, the Spirit of truth, unites, enlightens, energises,
and activates our new minds to do the will of God and binds us in
a spiritual, brotherly relationship with Jesus and all other believers.

What an amazing array of blessings God bestows on those who love him. God declares that we are his children, and as a result, God's truths are written on the hearts and minds of all believers, and Jesus asks the Father to send God's Spirit to live in us and guide us.

Far from being an only child, Jesus is my brother, God is my Father, and millions of believers both before me and after me are my brothers and sisters. What a transformation for an only child!

MEDITATION – MY BROTHER

- Read (not sing!) through the words of the following hymn. Identify how the writer captures the truths of the gospel.

- Do you have brothers or sisters in your family? What is your relationship with them? Could your relationship with your brother Jesus improve your relationship with your earthly brother or sister?

- Have you thought of Jesus as your brother and sharing the same familial relationship with the Father? How does that make you feel?

- Today, there are millions of Christian brothers and sisters living around the world. In fact, about one and a half to two billion. So even if we feel isolated sometimes, there is no need to do so.

- You can get inspiration on how Jesus is building his universal church at www.gafcon/prayer. If you can, have a look now.

- Do you recognise a special bond with other believers? How is it different from other relationships?

- Do you feel the Holy Spirit directing your thoughts at times – enlightening, inspiring, correcting?

- Use the link or code to listen to the choir sing the hymn and thank God that Jesus is your brother.

https://open.spotify.com/track/5n3StDhKZiGXs91GQpcZ66?si=cafcc310e141458d

BREATHE ON ME BREATH OF GOD

Breathe on me, breath of God,
fill me with life anew,
that I may love all that you love
and do what you would do.

Breath on me breath of God,
until my heart is pure,
until with you I will one will,
to do and to endure.

Breathe on me, breath of God
and all my life refine,
until this earthly part of me
glows with your fire divine.

Breathe on me, breath of God,
so shall I never die,
but live with you the perfect life
of your eternity.

Edwin Hatch

My Friend

'What A Friend We Have In Jesus'

I am fortunate to have several good friends with whom I enjoy mutual affection and regard. We acknowledge each other as friends. Some are friends because of mutual interests; others simply because we enjoy each other's company and natures. Our friendships are not based on any obligations other than to be the other's friend.

But I find that having Jesus as my friend is very different.

One of the great joys of having a good friend is that, as the friendship grows, I can share with them my highs, my lows, my questions, my uncertainties; in fact almost any aspect of my life. And they can do the same with me. But I am prepared to admit that somewhere in my life I have matters that I will not share even with a very best friend. Why? Simply because I am not sure that those aspects of my life may be acceptable to my friend, and that will be the end of the friendship. But with Jesus, I can be completely candid. In fact, I must be - Jesus knows me completely! Jesus is the friend who knows me through and through - better than I know myself! And a friend who not only knows me, but will accept me as I am, even the parts of my life of which I am ashamed. He may not like those parts, but he mercifully accepts me as I am, completely naked before him. There is no other friend like that.

And unlike my other friends, Jesus is always accessible. I'm sure that, like me, you have been in a position where you would appreciate the advice of a friend, or you have something you want to share with them. You contact them, phone, text, email, anything, and they are just not available. How frustrating! How annoying! But Jesus is there – always, twenty-four/seven. And my access to him is immediate and he knows me through and through.

And Jesus is my friend who sits at the right hand of God the Father Almighty. How amazing is that! To have a friend with direct access to the creator. But also, a little scary. God has made it clear in his word that he is not like us, his ways are not our ways, and his thoughts are not our thoughts. He is holy and pure and his face we cannot see. But Jesus, my friend, is with the Father and he has told me that whatever I ask in his name, he will take to the Father on my behalf. And I know he will be gentle with me and present my feeble, sometimes misguided, requests appropriately.

Above all that, Jesus is my friend because in obedience to his Father's will, he gave his life for me so that I could have a relationship with the Father and a life everlasting. What a friend! But, as I said before, friendship is a mutual relationship. Both parties must acknowledge the friendship. I do want to have Jesus as my friend because of what he has done for me and all believers.

But will he acknowledge me as his friend?

Of the spoken words of Jesus that are recorded in the four gospels, Jesus uses the word 'friend' rarely. And, in most cases, it is when he is telling a parable or a story, as in the comparison between his ministry and that of John the Baptist (Matthew 11:18-19), or in the parable of the workers in the vineyard (Matthew 20:13-16), or the parable of the wedding banquet (Matthew 22:1-12), and several other similar instances.

On only five occasions does he directly address a person or persons as 'friend'. Judas was addressed as 'friend' when he betrayed Jesus (Matthew 26:50) and no doubt this was Jesus at his sardonic best. He called the recently dead Lazarus his friend on his way to his tomb, and we are told how much he loved Lazarus and his friendship (John 11:11). On the other three occasions, he was addressing the disciples. Once, when instructing the disciples on the hypocrisy of the Pharisees (Luke 12:4-5), once when inviting the disciples to join him for breakfast after his resurrection (John 21:5), and, most importantly, when he talks about those who would be his friends. So, we should pay close attention to this latter occasion to understand what Jesus expects of his friends.

After celebrating the Passover and before his arrest, Jesus comforted the disciples with many words including the following.

> *"My command is this: Love each other as I have loved you. Greater love has no one than this: to lay down one's life for one's friends. You are my friends if you do what I command. I no longer call you servants, because a servant does not know his master's business. Instead, I have called you friends, for everything that I learned from my Father I have made known to you. You did not choose me, but I chose you and appointed you so that you might go and bear fruit—fruit that will last—and so that whatever you ask in my name the Father will give you. This is my command: Love each other."* (John 15:12-17)

Jesus is asking the disciples, and through belief and faith all believers, to love other believers, even to the point of death. Why does he emphasise this so strongly? In the previous meditation, 'My Brother', we considered the prayer that Jesus prayed for all believers. Jesus prayed that *'that they may be brought to complete unity. Then the world will know that you sent me and have loved them even as you have loved me.'* The operative word is 'then'. As a leader, Jesus knew that the unity of believers was the key to the proclamation of the gospel and the growth of his church. And for unity to be unbreakable, love between believers is the essential element.

That does not seem a problem - after all, we are talking about fellow brothers and sisters. But it can be so easy for that love to fray or dissipate: that person with a loud voice who sits behind you in church and can't hold a tune; the sermon that has reached forty minutes and is only at point two of five; the friend who was to meet for coffee and prayer and forgot the appointment; the person who agrees to take on a regular task but only performs every other time; and so on. These little things can stretch a friendship. But there can be bigger issues when questions of doctrine and belief are at stake. All annoyances, differences and disagreements can put love to the test, and if love fails, the unity of Christ's church is compromised.

So, as I rejoice to call Jesus 'my friend', I must do my best to obey his command to 'love each other' unconditionally as he exampled.

MEDITATION – MY FRIEND

• Read (not sing!) through the words of the following hymn. Identify how the writer captures the truths of the gospel.

• Do you have good friends? What is the basis of one of those friendships?

• How does your friendship with Jesus differ from that of your earthly friends?

• Is there a danger of becoming too familiar with Jesus as a friend? How can you prevent that?

• Do you find some other believers difficult to befriend? Why? What is the solution? Do you have a particular example? What could you do? Consider Paul's words in 1 Corinthians 13.

• Among all his other attributes, do you see Jesus as a leader? Give some examples from the gospels.

• Use the link or code to listen to the choir sing the hymn and thank God that Jesus is your friend.

https://open.spotify.com/track/0h198SKmXY53w1jog0ZGH0?si=c48def78be99497d

WHAT A FRIEND WE HAVE IN JESUS

What a friend we have in Jesus
all our sins and griefs to bear,
what a privilege to carry
everything to God in prayer:
O what peace we often forfeit,
O what needless pain we bear,
all because we do not carry
everything to God in prayer.

Have we trials and temptations,
is there trouble anywhere?
we should never be discouraged:
take it to the Lord in prayer.
Can we find a friend so faithful
who will all our sorrows share?
Jesus knows our every weakness:
take it to the Lord in prayer.

Are we weak and heavy laden,
cumbered with a load of care?
Jesus is our only refuge
take it to the Lord in prayer.
Do your friends despise, forsake you?
Take it to the Lord in prayer
in his arms he'll take and shield you,
You will find a solace there.

Joseph Medlicott Scriven

My Prophet

'Guide Me, O Thou Great Redeemer'

Prophets were always a part of God's relationship with his chosen people from the time of Moses until Jesus, God's final prophet. Their predictions proved unerringly true for both Israel and the surrounding nations. There were also false prophets, but God used their deceitful predictions in his plan of salvation.

During his earthly ministry, you could almost call Jesus the 'accidental prophet'. 'Accidental' as, being God, he always knew how events were going to play out in the context of his statements about future events. There are many examples including the following: the raising of Jairus' daughter (Mark 5:35-43); the surprising haul of fish (Luke 5:1-11); the royal official's son (John 4:46-53); his own death and resurrection (Mark 9:30-32); Peter's denial (Mark 14:27-31). Apart from such prophesies that were fulfilled during Jesus' lifetime, after Jesus' resurrection, only three of his prophesies remained unfulfilled: that believers would be gifted the Holy Spirit, that the four-hundred-year-old Jerusalem temple would be destroyed, and his prophesy about the end of the age.

However, apart from the real-life situations such as those above, many of the words of Jesus fall into the realm of prophesy for us today. Matthew's gospel has some examples.

In the Sermon on the Mount (Matthew 5:1 – 7:29), Jesus predicts many outcomes. In the first eleven verses, Jesus prophesises the future outcome of certain behaviours. Those who are meek will inherit the earth; those who are merciful will be shown mercy; and so on. Finally, those who receive hatred because of their faithfulness to Jesus will receive great reward in heaven. He then goes on to speak about how God measures our behaviour in several real-life circumstances: murder, adultery, divorce, oaths, and so on. At the end of the sermon (Matthew 7:24-27), he tells his hearers that putting his words into practice will result in them building their spiritual house, and eternal life, on a rock that will stand, whereas ignoring his words will end up with their house built on sand, crashing around their ears.

When the disciples were having difficulty healing a boy with a demon (Matthew 17:14-21), Jesus told them they had too little faith. He went on to explain that with just a little quality faith, nothing would be impossible for them. The same applies to us today . Later, he went on to talk about forgiveness using the parable of the unmer- ciful servant (Matthew 18:21-35). In verse thirty-five, Jesus predicts that unmerciful behaviour in this life will be viewed unfavourably by God the Father.

In the parable of the talents (Matthew 25:14-30), Jesus explains that everyone has gifts that we should use in God's service. Some people have more than others, but if a person fails to use the gifts that God has given them, they will at a future time incur God's wrath and condemnation. In a similar way, we are all capable of generosity towards those who are worse off than we are. In the story of the sheep and the goats (Matthew 25:31-46), Jesus foretells that those who do not practice hospitality, especially to God's people, will in the end go to eternal punishment, but those who are righteous will go to eternal life.

Returning to Jesus' prophesy of the end of the age, the gospels of Matthew, Mark and Luke all contain the words of Jesus' end of the age prophesy. The accounts are similar in both content and emphasis. The major themes of the prophesy lay out the environment that believers should expect to encounter leading up to the end of the age: aggression and wars between nations; severe natural disasters, such as earthquakes and famines; disturbances and chaos in the heavenly bodies; the appearances of false prophets and false messiahs; love dissipating among believers and many turning from their faith; infighting, rebellion, and treachery within families; hatred and persecution of believers.

Aggression and wars between nations, severe natural disasters such as earthquakes and famines, and disturbances and chaos in the heavenly bodies are global, cosmic matters that are outside my control and that I can do nothing about. In most cases, they are outside the control of mankind, although there is some evidence that mankind thinks we can have some influence. In fact, many similar events were happening as Jesus uttered the prophesy and have been happening ever since. Jesus does emphasise the severity of the events, so perhaps we should expect to see such events intensify as the end draws nearer. The point is that Jesus is letting me know that things are not going to get any better as far as the state of the natural world and mankind's relationships with each other. But I know from his promises that he will keep me safe in his own way, so I'm going to leave these global matters up to him and pray for mercy for those who are affected.

But the other elements of the prophesy are matters that could affect me and over which I have some control: the appearances of false prophets and false messiahs; love dissipating among believers and many turning from their faith; infighting, rebellion, and treachery within families; hatred and persecution of believers. With God's help I can plan for, pray about, and have a response in each case.

Surprisingly, there is one aspect of this prophecy that Jesus said he has no control over and no knowledge of - when will the end come? Jesus tells us that no one knows, not even the angels or the Son, but only the Father. And so, in four parables he emphasises the need to be ready and watch either for the end of the world, or prepared for our own death: the watchful servants (Mark 13:32-37); another watchful servant (Matthew 24:45-51); the ten virgins (Matthew 25:1-13); the rich fool (Luke 12:16-21). Reading God's word regularly can help us be watchful and control our lives.

But my favourite prophesy is also a wonderful promise. Jesus was addressing the disciples, and I am sure his words apply to all believers.

> *"Do not let your hearts be troubled. You believe in God; believe also in me. My Father's house has many rooms; if that were not so, would I have told you that I am going there to prepare a place for you? And if I go and prepare a place for you, I will come back and take you to be with me that you also may be where I am. You know the way to the place where I am going."* (John 14:1-4)

Today we have a rather cynical view of prophets; their predictions are wrong more often than right. Think weather forecasters or economic gurus. But the beautiful thing about Jesus' prophesies is that they can be relied on and, for that reason, give me and all believers a sure and certain hope.

MEDITATION – MY PROPHET

- Read (not sing!) through the words of the following hymn. Identify how the writer captures the truths of the gospel.

- Have you ever thought of Jesus as a prophet? Explain.

- Can you think of other examples where Jesus' words were prophetic?

- What do you think of when you read Jesus' prophecy of the end of the age?

- Does Jesus' end of the age prophecy give you hope or despair?

- What do you do to be watchful and ready? You can get some idea from Paul's letter to Timothy – 2 Timothy 3:1-9.

- Do you have a favourite prophecy of Jesus? What is it?

- Use the link or code to listen to the choir sing the hymn and thank God that Jesus is your prophet.

https://open.spotify.com/track/1bCthQoeh1Iw8oDIoAdBuN?si=39b9a63fc3554d43

GUIDE ME, O THOU GREAT REDEEMER

Guide me, O thou great Redeemer,
pilgrim through this barren land;
I am weak, but thou art mighty;
hold me with thy powerful hand:
bread of heaven, bread of heaven,
feed me now and evermore,
feed me now and evermore.

Open now the crystal fountain
whence the living waters flow:
let the fiery, cloudy pillar
lead me all my journey through:
strong deliverer, strong deliverer,
be thou still my strength and shield,
be thou still my strength and shield.

When I tread the verge of Jordan
bid my anxious fears subside;
death of death, and hell's destruction,
land me safe on Canaan's side:
songs of praises, songs of praises
I will ever give to thee,
I will ever give to thee.

William Williams

My Priest

'Jesus, The Very Thought Of Thee'

For me, there are four pivotal points in the story of God's people and at each point the following are present - sacrifice, substitution, blood, salvation and priests.

When Isaac had grown to be a young man, God instructed Abraham to sacrifice him as a test of Abraham's commitment (Genesis 22:1-19). The story tells us that at the crucial moment, God provided a ram for the sacrifice. In this instance, the ram was a substitution sacrifice in place of Isaac. Blood was shed, and Isaac was saved. God reiterated and expanded his previous amazing promises to Abraham, but this time with an oath and told him that he now knew that Abraham feared, or revered, him. In a sense, God was the priest overseeing the whole event.

Later, at the time of the Exodus, God gave Moses instructions for the Israelites so that they would be protected from God's last plague when God's 'destroyer' would pass through the land of Egypt, killing the firstborn of every family (Exodus 12). Those instructions were for a special meal to be prepared on the night of the Exodus. A lamb was to be selected on the tenth day of the month and then four days later, killed. The blood was to be sprinkled on the sides and tops of the doorframes of each Israeli house. These houses the destroyer would pass over. In this instance, the lamb substituted for the first born, it was sacrificed and its blood a sign that the first born and its household would be untouched. As with the previous example, God acted as priest.

After God had led the Israelites out of Egypt, he established a covenant with them at Mount Sinai: he would be their God and they would be his chosen people, a holy nation. The covenant was to be sustained by three outward signs: a group of laws including the Ten Commandments, the creation of five offerings by which the people could thank God for his mercies or, in the case of sin, obtain atonement through the sacrifice of an unblemished animal. And the establishment of a priesthood that would administer the sacrificial process and act as mediators between the people and God.

While on the mountain with God, God told Moses to build a sanctuary where he would dwell among the Israelites. He also gave Moses detailed instructions on how the sanctuary was to be built and furnished, instructions on how the priests who would administer the tabernacle were to be dressed, how they were to be consecrated, and how the sacrifices were to be performed. He chose Aaron and his tribe, the Levites, to be set apart as priests.

God's instructions to Moses are very detailed and precise. He didn't say 'make an alter', or 'make a sacrifice', but gave exact dimensions, designs and procedures for every item. The detail emphasised to Moses, the Israelites, and to us today, what a holy God we worship. It is also another proof statement for the authenticity of the Bible: the detail in Chapters 35 to 39 of Exodus are precise and unique.

Details for the various sacrifices can be found in Chapters 1 to 7 of Leviticus. In the case of sacrifices for sins, the individual would bring a lamb without defect to the temple. He would place his hand on the head of the animal, symbolising the transfer of his sin to the animal, as substitution for himself. He would then kill it in front of the priest. The priest would then take the blood and sprinkle it on various items in the temple. The priest cut off the fatty portions and burnt them to create an aroma pleasing to the Lord. The process was an act of atonement for the sin of the individual with the priest mediating between the sinner and God.

However, during the five to six hundred years of Israelite history following the establishment of the temple sacrifices, it became clear that the priests were not performing their tasks in a way that honoured God and the people were not obeying God's commands as he intended and were acting with malice toward others. The covenant with its commandments, sacrifices and priests was not working. The prophets noted God's displeasure (Malachi 1:8 and Hosea 6:6) which finally resulted in the Israelites exile at the hands of the Assyrians and Babylonians and the end of the nation of Israel.

At the same time as Israel was drawing away from God, the prophets were announcing cosmic shifts to the relationship between mankind and God. God would initiate a new covenant with the house of Israel (Jeremiah 31:31-34), and a suffering servant would appear who, in a paradoxical way, would make atonement for sin (Isaiah 52:13- 53:12).

> *"We all, like sheep, have gone astray, each of us has turned*
> *to our own way;*
> > *and the Lord has laid on him the iniquity of us all."*
> (Isaiah 53:6)

And the writer of Hebrews, interpreting Messianic prophesies in Psalms 2 and 110, shows that God applies to Jesus the role of high priest but of a different line than Aaron's.

> *"In the same way, Christ did not take on himself the glory*
> *of becoming a high priest. But God said to him, "You are*
> *my Son; today I have become your Father."*
>
> *And he says in another place, "You are a priest forever,*
> *in the order of Melchizedek."* (Hebrews 5:5-6)

Hundreds of years later, when Jesus began his ministry and came to the Jordan where John was baptising, John announced, *"Look, the Lamb of God, who takes away the sin of the world."* (John 1:29)

In Jesus' Passion all the elements of the previous sacrifices are repeated, but this time on a cosmic, supernatural scale. Just as the lamb was taken to the temple by sinners, so Jesus was taken to, and nailed to, the cross by sinners. But, unlike the sinner at the temple transferring his sin by laying his hand on the head of his lamb, the LORD transferred the sin of the world to Jesus, the Lamb of God. But this was no symbolic act as at the temple: now the full iniquity of the world, the sin of the world, from creation to the end of time, was transferred to Jesus and, as the prophet says, it was the LORD'S will to crush him and cause him to suffer (Isaiah 53:10). It is not possible to frame Jesus' agony with human words. It is as if, for a moment in time, one member of the Trinity was absent. What immeasurable pain that must have brought to the Father and the Spirit.

As the unimaginable weight of that accumulated sin bore down on Jesus, his intimate relationship with his Father disappeared and he cried out in mortal anguish.

> *"At noon, darkness came over the whole land until three*
> *in the afternoon. And at three in the afternoon Jesus*
> *cried out in a loud voice, "Eloi, Eloi, lama sabachthani?"*

*(which means "My God, my God, why have you forsaken
me?").* (Mark 15:33-34)

Mercifully, shortly after, like the lamb at the temple, Jesus died.
And, just as the high priest in the temple sprinkled the blood of the
sinner's lamb on temple articles, so the blood of Jesus, God's High
Priest, and the Lamb of God, was sprinkled on the cross. Just as with
the animal at the temple, the transfer of sin, sacrifice, and the sprin-
kling of blood, brought forgiveness to the sinner, so Jesus, through
his death, brings forgivness for all who believe.

> *"For God so loved the world that he gave his one and
> only Son, that whoever believes in him shall not perish
> but have eternal life. For God did not send his Son into
> the world to condemn the world, but to save the world
> through him. Whoever believes in him is not condemned,
> but whoever does not believe stands condemned already
> because they have not believed in the name of God's one
> and only Son."* (John3:16-18)

But, unlike the animal and the priest at the temple who must
repeat the act of sacrifice and mediation over and over again, Jesus'
subsequent resurrection and ascension to the Father's right hand
assures us that we have a High Priest who continues to act on our
behalf.

> *"Now there have been many of those priests, since death
> prevented them from continuing in office; but because
> Jesus lives forever, he has a permanent priesthood.
> Therefore he is able to save completely those who come to*

God through him, because he always lives to intercede for them." (Hebrews 7:23-25)

Perhaps all we have considered above, and Jesus' role as priest, can be best summarised by the beautiful prayer said before The Communion in the 1662 Book of Common Prayer that echoes the Canaanite woman's heartfelt faith.

"We do not presume to come to this thy Table, O Merciful Lord, trusting in our own righteousness, but in thy manifold and great mercies. We are not worthy so much as to gather up the crumbs under thy Table. But thou art the same Lord, whose property is always to have mercy: Grant us therefore, gracious Lord, so to eat the flesh of thy dear Son Jesus Christ, and to drink his blood, that our sinful bodies may be made clean by his body, and our souls washed through his most precious blood, and that we may evermore dwell in him, and he in us. Amen."

Over two thousand years ago Jesus died for the sins of the entire world once and for all. What a blessing it is to know that today, when I repent and believe, my eternal High Priest - Jesus, who all those years ago paid the price for my sins, lives and is alive. And when I fall, he will intercede and mediate for me and draw me close to God.

MEDITATION – MY PRIEST

- Read (not sing!) through the words of the following hymn. Identify how the writer captures the truths of the gospel.

- Substitution, sacrifice, and blood are key elements in the examples of salvation we have looked at. How is the outcome different in each case?

- Why did God give such detailed instructions to Moses on laws and sacrifices? How should it influence our relationship with God today?

- Why do you think the sacrifices that God instituted did not solve the problem of sin?

- Have you ever pondered how the 'iniquity of us all' would have weighed on Jesus as he hung on the cross? Do so now – just for your own sins. Then imagine how it would have been for the 'sin of the world'.

- What other cataclysmic events happened at the moment of Jesus' death? How do they confirm the significance of Jesus' death?

- Use the link or code to listen to the choir sing the hymn and thank God that Jesus is your priest.

https://open.spotify.com/track/6RQgvHzNVaRm5ManPOLI3v?si=6c0beaae637f47bf

JESUS THE VERY THOUGHT OF THEE

Jesus, the very thought of thee
with sweetness fills the breast;
but sweeter far thy face to see,
and in thy presence rest.

Nor voice can sing, nor heart can frame,
Nor can the memory find
A sweeter sound than Thy blest Name,
O Savior of mankind!

O hope of every contrite heart,
O joy of all the meek,
to those who fall, how kind thou art!
how good to those who seek!

But what to those who find? Ah, this
nor tongue nor pen can show;
the love of Jesus, what it is,
none but his loved ones know.

Jesus, our only joy be thou,
as thou our prize wilt be;
Jesus, be thou our glory now,
and through eternity.

Attributed to: St Bernard of Clairvaux Psalm 104:34

BEHOLD THE LAMB OF GOD

Behold the Lamb of God,
that taketh away the sin of the world

George Frederic Handel

https://open.spotify.com/track/5T8FNok2ijbcYp3mNA0G8p?si=7b029d99ab7b4b39

My King

'O Worship The King All-Glorious Above'

Jesus, the obedient Son, never gave himself the title of king. That title was announced by four people who, at the time, had little or no prior contact with Jesus. There were the Magi who came seeking the *'king of the Jews'* (Matthew 2:1-2). Then the God-fearing Israelite Nathanael declared, *'you are the king of Israel'* (John 1:43-51). Then the crowd, who days later would demand his crucifixion, called out, *'blessed is the king'* (Luke 19:37-40). Finally, Pilate who, when under pressure from the Jews, did not back away from the inscription he had placed on the cross, *'JESUS OF NAZARETH THE KING OF THE JEWS'* (John 19:19-22). Was the Spirit at work, giving people from all walks of life the insight that Jesus was God's king?

The history of the Israelites is a cautionary tale of the futility of ignoring God as king. Until we come to the book of Judges God was Israel's king, ruling the Israelites through a series of surrogates from Abraham through to Joshua. The book of Judges is a sad story of living with no king. On the death of Joshua and his contemporaries Israel fell into a period when they ignored God, debased the priest-hood and worshipped the gods of the surrounding people. During this period of over three-hundred years, God had to intervene many times to keep the Israelites from self-annihilation. It was a time of self-centred selfishness. The situation is succinctly recorded four times in Judges.

> *"In those days Israel had no king; everyone did as they as they saw fit."* (Judges 17:6, 21:25)

At the end of this three-hundred-year period, God called the prophet-priest Samuel to lead Israel. Samuel re-established a reverence for God, won a resounding victory against the Philistines, and brough stability and strength to Israel. Towards the end of Samuel's long life, the people asked him to give them a king like the other nations.

Samuel appointed Saul as the first king, but he disobeyed God's instructions given through Samuel, and God told Samuel to move on and appoint a second king, David. Following David's death, his son Solomon became king. Then when Israel became a divided nation, there were twenty-two kings of the Northern Kingdom and twenty of the Southern Kingdom.

Four hundred years earlier, when Moses was addressing the Israelites prior to his death he foresaw that at some time future generations would ask for a king and gave this advice.

> *"When he takes the throne of his kingdom, he is to write for himself on a scroll a copy of this law, taken from that of the Levitical priests. It is to be with him, and he is to read it all the days of his life so that he may learn to revere the Lord his God and follow carefully all the words of this law and these decrees."* (Deuteronomy 17:18-19)

But, of the forty-five kings of the two kingdoms only eight did right in God's sight and only one, Josiah, paid close attention to the Law as Moses had directed. How surprising! God had been their king for over five hundred years through the times of Abraham, Isaac, Jacob , Joseph, Moses, and Joshua. Now they were opting for worldly solutions to their problems. During this time had God ever let them down? No. Had God reneged on his promises? No. Had God ever forgotten them? No.

Over an eight-hundred-year period we observe Israel without a king, and then with many kings. Unfortunately, in both cases the results are very similar, and we watch the Israelites drifting away from God, and God becoming more and more unhappy with their behaviour. Finally, God had become tired of their behaviour and prophesied their fate at the hand of the Assyrians and then the Babylonians.

> *"Hear this, you priests! Pay attention, you Israelites! Listen, royal house!*
>
> *This judgment is against you: You have been a snare at Mizpah, a net spread out on Tabor. The rebels are knee-deep in slaughter. I will discipline all of them. I know all about Ephraim; Israel is not hidden from me. Ephraim, you have now turned to prostitution; Israel is corrupt. Their deeds do not permit them to return to their God."* (Hosea 5:1-4)

But, with God there is always hope. The book of Ruth, coming after Judges, is a beautiful example of how some people choose to follow God's way in their lives even though the surrounding social and political environment, and the leaders, were in disarray and devoid of any recognition of God. And sandwiched between Nehemiah and Job, we find the book of Esther. Both books demonstrate that even in times when leaders and society ignore God he can still be worshipped and obeyed. It is, in a sense, like the situation that Christians in the West find themselves in today.

Later, the prophets were announcing the coming of a righteous king who would rule over all creation. In the face of mankind's futile efforts, God would take the initiative and establishes his chosen king.

> *"Rejoice greatly, Daughter Zion! Shout, Daughter Jerusalem! See, your king comes to you, righteous and victorious, lowly and riding on a donkey, on a colt, the foal of a donkey. I will take away the chariots from Ephraim and the warhorses from Jerusalem, and the battle bow will be broken. He will proclaim peace to the nations. His rule will extend from sea to sea and from the River to the ends of the earth."* (Zechariah 9:9-10)

Although he never called himself king, Jesus makes it clear that he is the king of the Father's kingdom when speaking to the disciples.

> *"And I confer on you a kingdom, just as my Father conferred one on me, so that you may eat and drink at my table in my kingdom and sit on thrones, judging the twelve tribes of Israel."* (Luke 22:29-30)

Jesus spoke about the kingdom more than any other matter: the kingdom where he is king. At one time when the disciples were concerned by earthly matters Jesus told them not to worry about earthly matters but to seek first the Father's kingdom (Luke 12:22-31). He told them that searching for the kingdom was the most important thing they could do, like people behave when they are intent on acquiring something of great value (Matthew 13:44-46).

On many occasions Jesus said that the kingdom is near (Matthew 4:17). Perhaps he said that because he was present, in person, or perhaps it was because they did not have to expend physical effort to seek the kingdom. Paul, when speaking about belief and faith in Jesus made this point (Romans 10:5-13 referencing Deuteronomy 30:11-14). And Jesus, in his conversation with the then uncomprehending Nicodemus, made it clear that the kingdom must be understood and accepted as a spiritual experience (John 3:1-21).

When we place our faith in Jesus' death and resurrection we are, so to speak, on the outskirts of the kingdom: we have the basic building blocks we need for the kingdom, and our spirit begins to commune with God's Spirit.

From time-to-time Jesus gave examples of behaviour in this life that would be worthy of the kingdom (Matthew 5:10, Matthew 18:1-4, Luke 6:20). He also described behaviour that could hinder inclusion in the kingdom (Mark 10:17-27, Luke 9:57-62).

It can be easy to live life like the people in the time of the Judges: a self-indulgence that satisfies us and puts us as the centre of everything and excludes others and God. Or we can follow man-made or appointed 'kings' that ignore God and are hostile to Jesus.

Thank God for his mercy in giving me the opportunity to accept Jesus as my king and to be able to look forward to the final chapters of Revelation, when Jesus will appear on a white horse with the following inscription on his robe and thigh.

"KING OF KINGS AND LORD OF LORDS" (Revelation 19:16)

Until that time, Jesus has promised (Matthew 28:18-20) to be my king in this life and to eternity.

MEDITATION – MY KING

- Read (not sing!) through the words of the following hymn. Identify how the writer captures the truths of the gospel.

- From the time of the Judges the Bible paints a grim picture of mankind's relationship with God. But there are periods when hope is glimpsed. What are those times? What was the difference?

- Find time to read the book of Ruth – it only takes about 20 minutes.

- What changed with the life, death, and resurrection of Jesus?

- On several occasions in the gospels, we read that the people wanted to make Jesus their king. What were their motives? How did Jesus respond?

- There are many other times when Jesus spoke about the kingdom. Search out three or four more.

- How did Jesus exhibit the attributes of a godly king?

- Do you hope for a future in Jesus' heavenly kingdom?

- Use the link or code to listen to the choir sing the hymn and thank God that Jesus is your king.

https://open.spotify.com/track/3Z9JejINiDCxiYyUU1xBqw?si=9930cc125d254f20

O WORSHIP THE KING ALL-GLORIOUS ABOVE

O worship the King, all-glorious above,
O gratefully sing his power and his love:
our shield and defender, the ancient of days,
pavilioned in splendour, and girded with praise.

O tell of his might, O sing of his grace,
whose robe is the light, whose canopy space;
his chariots of wrath the deep thunder-clouds form,
and dark is his path on the wings of the storm.

The earth with its store of wonders untold,
Almighty, your power has founded of old,
established it fast by a changeless decree,
and round it has cast, like a mantle, the sea.

Your bountiful care what tongue can recite?
it breathes in the air, it shines in the light,
it streams from the hills, it descends to the plain,
and sweetly distils in the dew and the rain.

Frail children of dust, and feeble as frail,
in you do we trust, nor find you to fail:
your mercies how tender, how firm to the end,
our maker, defender, redeemer and friend.

O measureless might, ineffable love,
while angels delight to hymn you above,
the humbler creation, though faltering their praise,
with true adoration shall sing all their days.

Robert Grant

My Lord

'All Hail The Power Of Jesus' Name'

I am sure that if I had been alive when Jesus walked the earth, I would have been a disciple in the line of Thomas. I have a disposition to being impulsive and a bit of a sceptic. If these characteristics seem contrary, the life of Thomas shows otherwise. Poor Thomas has received the designation of, in my view unfairly, 'doubting Thomas' and this sobriquet is often applied to those who question 'settled' opinion on any matter.

Thomas was one of the initial twelve disciples, as we see from reference to him just before Jesus' Sermon on the Mount (Luke 6:12-16) and in the sending out of the disciples to preach the gospel in the surrounding villages (Matthew 10:3). The next time we meet Thomas he shows his impulsive, but loyal and courageous nature. When Jesus was told about the death of Lazarus he decided to return to Lazarus' home in an area where the Jews had just attempted to stone him. The other disciples tried to dissuade Jesus, but Thomas bravely supported Jesus (John 11:1-16).

Later, after Jesus had celebrated the Passover with the disciples and before his arrest, he told them that he would be with them for only a little longer. Naturally they become concerned and worried. Jesus told them not to be troubled.

> *"Do not let your hearts be troubled. You believe in God; believe also in me. My Father's house has many rooms; if that were not so, would I have told you that I am going there to prepare a place for you? And if I go and prepare a place for you, I will come back and take you to be with me that you also may be where I am. You know the way to the place where I am going."* (John 14:1-4).

It is unlikely that any of them fully understood. After all, Jesus, to this point, had not really told them the place and the way. But it was only Thomas who asked for clarification and, in doing so, became the catalyst for one of Jesus' longest and most profound teachings.

> *"Thomas said to him, "Lord, we don't know where you are going, so how can we know the way?"*
>
> *Jesus answered, "I am the way and the truth and the life. No one comes to the Father except through me. If you really know me, you will know my Father as well. From now on, you do know him and have seen him."* (John 14:5-7).

And, in the discourse that followed, Jesus summarised the purpose of his ministry and the mysteries of the gospel (John 14:7-16:28). When Jesus finished speaking, the disciples said that he had made everything clear to them and they now believed that he came from God. (John 16:29-30).

But perhaps Thomas' most compelling and insightful words were yet to come. Following the resurrection, the disciples were hiding in a locked room for fear of the Jews when Jesus came and stood among them, showed them his hands and side, breathed on them the Holy Spirit, and then departed. For some reason, Thomas was absent at the time and did not return for a week. We don't know where he was, but he had seven days to agonise over the thought that Jesus was dead. The disciples, on the other hand, only had to wait three days before seeing their resurrected leader.

When Thomas returned, you can imagine how excited the disciples would have been to tell him the good news that Jesus was alive. But Thomas?

> *"Now Thomas (also known as Didymus), one of the Twelve, was not with the disciples when Jesus came. So the other disciples told him, "We have seen the Lord!"*
>
> *But he said to them, "Unless I see the nail marks in his hands and put my finger where the nails were, and put my hand into his side, I will not believe."*
>
> *A week later his disciples were in the house again, and Thomas was with them. Though the doors were locked, Jesus came and stood among them and said, "Peace be with you!" Then he said to Thomas, "Put your finger here; see my hands. Reach out your hand and put it into my side. Stop doubting and believe."*
>
> *Thomas said to him, "My Lord and my God!"* (John 20:24-28).

Just when Thomas' scepticism and despair was at its height, Jesus arrives with the very proof that Thomas was demanding. What a moment!

During Jesus ministry, the disciples addressed him at times as 'Master'; at other times as 'Teacher', but usually as 'Lord'. They were convinced of Jesus' deity, had told him that they knew he came from God, had heard him use the term 'Son of God' of himself, and had been told that he was going to the Father. But they had not explicitly acknowledged him as God. Thomas in a flash of faith and spiritual inspiration made this powerful connection and confession. His Lord was his God!

Then Jesus, in what could be seen as a gentle rebuke of Thomas, said the most encouraging words for all who have believed ever since.

> *"Then Jesus told him, "Because you have seen me, you have believed; blessed are those who have not seen and yet have believed."* (John 20:29)

And there are good reasons to 'believe without seeing'. During the four to five weeks following Jesus' crucifixion there are three events that are powerful proof statements for the truth of the gospel record.

First, a man died a horrific death and then was alive three days later. Imagine if you had seen someone die and reappear from the dead. You would certainly want to tell people about it. Hardly an event you would keep a secret. On the other hand, if you had seen someone die only, well, that happens every day.

Second, consider the disciples' behaviour following Jesus' resurrection. They became galvanised and their actions were quite remarkable. They spent the rest of their lives telling all they could about the salvation that could be found by faith in the death and resurrection of Jesus. They risked their careers, their personal lives, and in most cases their physical lives. These men were ordinary people; most of them simple, uneducated fishermen, yet their writings are of a very high theological and literary standard and although written without collaboration display remarkable consistency. Their message was unpopular; it was anathema to the Jews and a source of ridicule to others. Why would they behave as they did in the face of opposition and persecution? Their leader had been publicly humiliated, denounced as a criminal, and then executed in a barbaric fashion. When Jesus was arrested prior to his crucifixion all his followers fled and one who was to become a leader in the development of Christianity, Peter, denied he even knew Jesus when questioned. How did they become so powerful, courageous, and persuasive? Following the death of Jesus, there was no compulsion for them to carry his work forward. There was no leader to be followed. There was nothing material to be gained. They had every opportunity to fade away and return to their previous lives.

Third, as noted above, the power of the resurrection, coupled with the gift of the Holy Spirit, galvanized the disciples and the little mustard seed began to grow. Christianity spread like wildfire across the known world and remarkably, this phenomenon occurred without any direction for, or any need of, political, civil, or military action. More surprisingly, from the time Jesus commenced his teachings and gathered his disciples, just three years had elapsed. During this time, he created no personal writings, established no organisational structure, left no one as a designated replacement, and gave only one operational instruction to his followers. There is no record of any other person achieving such continuing outcomes with such scant preparation – the results are quite simply outside human experience.

We know from our own life experiences that such events and behaviours just 'don't happen by chance'. It is inconceivable that my Lord is just someone from an obscure village who happened to have a comprehensive grasp of Old Testament history and scriptural teaching, or an amazing healer, or a person with power over death and nature, or a sacrificial saviour for the sins of the whole world. No!

Jesus is my God who created the heavens and the earth and, in his mercy, invites me to have an eternal relationship with him and, though I have not seen him like Thomas, through faith in his word and the testimony of Thomas and the other disciples I can, like Thomas, confidently say, *'My Lord and my God!'*.

MEDITATION – MY LORD

- Read (not sing!) through the words of the following hymn. Identify how the writer captures the truths of the gospel.

- Are you a bit like Thomas? Would you call yourself a sceptic? Would you have acted like Thomas did in each case?

- Do you find the truths and the salvation that God offers just too simple and good to believe? Do you have doubts at times?

- What do you do to overcome those doubts?

- Read through some of the powerful orations that the disciples gave shortly after the resurrection.
  - Peter   Acts 2:14-41
  - Stephen   Acts 7:1-60
  - Paul   Acts 13:13-43

- What convinces you of the truths of the Bible?

- Can you estimate how many millions of people from the time of Thomas have believed Jesus' words?

"Then Jesus told him, 'Because you have seen me, you have believed; blessed are those who have not seen and yet have believed.'" (John 20:29)

- Use the link or code to listen to the choir sing the hymn and thank God that Jesus is your Lord.

ALL HAIL THE POWER OF JESUS' NAME

All hail the power of Jesus' name;
let angels prostrate fall;
bring forth the royal diadem
to crown him Lord of all.

Crown him, you martyrs of our God,
who from his alter call;
praise him whose way of pain you trod,
and crown him Lord of all.

As heirs of Israel's chosen race
and ransomed from the fall,
hail him who saves you by his grace,
and crown him Lord of all.

Sinners, whose love cannot forget
the wormwood and the gall,
go spread your treasures at his feet
and crown him Lord of all.

Let every tribe and every tongue
responsive to his call,
now shout in universal song
and crown him Lord of all.

Edward Perronet

My Life

'Jesus Bids Us Shine With A Clear, Pure Light

Unlike the other attributes of Jesus (shepherd, brother, friend and so on) this attribute is at the very heart of our relationship with Jesus. In fact, all the other attributes only become realities because of our affirmation that Jesus is 'my life'.

So, if, like John Newton, I want to claim all the attributes of Jesus that we are considering, I must respond to Jesus like Martha when Jesus was coming to Lazarus.

> "Lord," Martha said to Jesus, "if you had been here, my brother would not have died. But I know that even now God will give you whatever you ask."
>
> Jesus said to her, "Your brother will rise again."
>
> Martha answered, "I know he will rise again in the resurrection at the last day."
>
> Jesus said to her, "I am the resurrection and the life. The one who believes in me will live, even though they die; and whoever lives by believing in me will never die. Do you believe this?"

> *"Yes, Lord," she replied, "I believe that you are the Messiah, the Son of God, who is to come into the world."*
> (John 11:21-27)

What a glorious array of blessings flow when we make that confession. However sinful we may have been or may be, God counts us as sinless. We now can have a relationship with the Father. We are assured of eternal life from the point we believed, and we can look forward to the joys of heaven. And Jesus asks the Father to pour out his Spirit on us to help and guide us through our life. If ever there was an offer you couldn't refuse, surely this is it: life has dramatically changed! Paul speaks eloquently of this in two passages in Romans (Romans 5:1-11 and 8:1-17).

But how should my life respond to these amazing new circumstances? Surely, I must let Jesus shape my lived life and my character. But what should that new person look like? On several occasions Jesus tells the disciples to emulate his character and life. Today, believers must strive to do the same.

> *"When he had finished washing their feet, he put on his clothes and returned to his place. "Do you understand what I have done for you?" he asked them. "You call me 'Teacher' and 'Lord,' and rightly so, for that is what I am. Now that I, your Lord and Teacher, have washed your feet, you also should wash one another's feet. I have set you an example that you should do as I have done for you. Very truly I tell you, no servant is greater than his master, nor is a messenger greater than the one who sent*

him. Now that you know these things, you will be blessed if you do them." (John 13:12-17)

In our struggles to emulate Jesus, we are helped by the the fruits of the Spirit, that the Father gives us, and that Paul identifies in Galatians (Galatians 5:22-26): love, joy, peace, patience, kindness, goodness, faithfulness, and self-control. But what do we learn from Jesus' example?

Consider the time Jesus met the man with leprosy (Matthew 8:1-4). We know nothing about the man, except his agonising plea and his belief that Jesus could heal him. 'Lord, if you are willing, you can make me clean'. Jesus responded immediately. He didn't ask for the man's medical history or any background. Spontaneously, Jesus showed his *compassion*. Am I always so inclined when I hear a cry for help?

Early in Jesus' ministry at a wedding banquet, Jesus solved an embarrassing situation, even though he was not ready to disclose his amazing powers (John 2:1-11). But for some reason, Jesus' mother was concerned about the situation. Whatever the reason, Jesus very graciously stepped in to solve the problem. Do I act *graciously* when something unexpected puts my plans in reverse?

Before he began his ministry, Jesus spent forty days and nights being tempted by the devil in the wilderness (Matthew 4:1-11). I suppose there are many words or actions with which Jesus could have answered the three temptations the devil put to him. However, in each case he responded with words that God gave Moses to say to the Israelites when they were being given the Law. In doing so, he demonstrated to the devil, and to us, that he is God, and, like God, he is *holy and righteous*. I too can use Jesus' approach by responding to the devil by using God's word. So, a good knowledge of God's word and its truths will be an important part of my growth.

When Jesus was approached by a Canaanite woman whose daughter was demon-possessed, he did not send her away, as the disciples had urged, but impressed with her sincere faith, *mercifully* granted her request (Matthew 15:21-28). Do I show mercy to those who are marginalised?

When a sinful woman poured expensive perfume on his feet, Jesus could have given in to the objections that were raised by his host and other guests (Luke 7:36-50). But he chose to ignore the implied criticism and spoke of the real meaning of *forgiveness* in his words and actions. Do I stand by my principals when under pressure?

In Jesus' great and final discourse with the disciples, he explained that his *love* was that of the Father (John 15:9-17:26); a love that is grounded in mercy and obedience. Can I aspire to love of that nature until I am made perfect? No, but I can try!

Before he was arrested, Jesus prayed to his Father… first for himself, then for the disciples and then for all believers. In his prayer for himself he summarized the work the Father had sent him to do and that he had completed that work. He had remained *faithful* to that task (John 17:1-5). Jesus expects me to show the same faithfulness.

During Jesus' ministry, the disciples witnessed many miracles and heard many parables, but they still were a bit slow in getting Jesus' message and objective. Jesus was very *patient* with them and stuck with them – although there were times nevertheless when his patience must have been tested (Matthew 15:10-20). Am I so patient when others don't share my ideas?

To summarise: faithful, loving, forgiving, merciful, holy, righteous, compassionate, and patient. The same character traits we see

God displaying as he led the Israelites throughout their history from Abram to Jesus.

But there is much more to consider when Jesus shapes my life. When speaking of his role as a shepherd (John 10:1-21), Jesus said that his sheep would have life to the full.

> *"I am the gate; whoever enters through me will be saved. They will come in and go out, and find pasture. The thief comes only to steal and kill and destroy; I have come that they may have life, and have it to the full."* (John 10:9-10)

Later he said that his followers would have the light of life.

> *"When Jesus spoke again to the people, he said, "I am the light of the world. Whoever follows me will never walk in darkness, but will have the light of life."* (John 8:12)

What wonderful promises! But there is also a responsibility and, in The Sermon on the Mount, Jesus made it clear that his followers were to display their light to the world through their life.

> *"You are the light of the world. A town built on a hill cannot be hidden. Neither do people light a lamp and put it under a bowl. Instead they put it on its stand, and it gives light to everyone in the house. In the same way, let your light shine before others, that they may see your good deeds and glorify your Father in heaven."* (Matthew5:14-16)

How can we ensure our life become the light that Jesus expects it to be?

Jesus knows very well the pitfalls that can prevent people from believing in him, absorbing his word, following his example, and growing more like him day by day. What tactics can the devil employ in my here and now life to diminish my growth and dim my light? What do I need to be prepared for and guard against?

In the Sermon on the Mount, Jesus gave several examples of behaviour that can distract us from belief and obedience. He highlighted the danger of being overcome by the lure of, and love of, riches and how chasing after money can draw us away from serving God (Matthew 6:19-24).

Because money is something that is so important to our life, and we spend a lot of time worrying about our finances, Jesus went on to explain that worry itself can be a distraction from serving God. Drawing on the beauty of the natural world that God created, he explained how futile worry about anything can be. God has our life, and in colloquial parlance, has our back, if we obey him and seek his kingdom (Matthew 6:25-34).

At another time, Jesus explained to the disciples that we should do all we can to prevent ourselves falling into sinful habits or for a sinful habit of ours to lead another believer to sin. Jesus' examples of how we should act are hyperbolic in the extreme, but the message is clear – 'flee from sin'. Perhaps that sin may be pride, or gambling, or drink, or sexual perversion, or laziness, or self-centredness. The message is clear - find a way to 'flee'!

There are many other examples of how we can brighten our light that come from Jesus' earthly ministry, and there is much helpful advice throughout the Bible, particularly in the Wisdom books of Job, Psalm, Ecclesiastes and Proverbs.

MEDITATION – MY LIFE

- Read (not sing!) through the words of the following hymn. Identify how the writer captures the truths of the gospel.

- The connection between a believer's life and light are constant themes in the Bible. Why?

- Are you always the 'light of the world'? What prevents our life from being that light?

- Do you make it a habit to dip into the wisdom books from time to time? How can they help you to keep on following Jesus?

- What other examples can you find in the Bible to brighten your light?

- What could you change in your life to increase the intensity of your light?

- Use the link or code to listen to the choir sing the hymn and thank God that Jesus is your life.

https://open.spotify.com/track/2jtTYEv7zqGlhCwG7jc6x1?si=1d98b0efae424dab

JESUS BIDS US SHINE

Jesus bids us shine,
With a clear, pure light,
Like a little candle burning in the night;
In this world of darkness, we must shine,
You in your small corner,
And I in mine.
Jesus bids us shine, first of all for Him
well He sees and knows it if our light grows dim;
He looks down from Heaven to see us shine
You in your small corner,
And I in mine.
Jesus bids us shine, then, for all around,
Many kinds of darkness in the world abound;
Sin and want and sorrow, so we must shine,
You in your small corner
And I in mine.
Jesus bids us shine as we work for Him,
Bringing those that wander
from the paths of sin;
He will ever help us if we shine,
You in your small corner,
And I in mine.

Susan Bogert Warner
Psalm 145

My Way

'Thou Art The Way'

'Way' is a small but ubiquitous word. It can be used in over forty different contexts, with quite different meanings! When the hymnwriter says Jesus is 'my way' I am assuming that he is using the word in the context of 'a method for obtaining an objective'. The objective is all the benefits that come from having a relationship with God the Father. Jesus says that he is the only way of achieving that outcome.

I do not know what statement of Jesus may have prompted the hymnwriter to assert that Jesus was 'my way' to the Father, but for me, it would have been the following response Jesus gave to Thomas when Thomas said he didn't know either where Jesus was going or the way. That response is perhaps one of the most controversial and powerful statements of Jesus' ministry.

Whichever statement it was, Newton was not going to be satisfied with the global statement 'the way'. He wanted it clear that, for him, Jesus was not just 'the way' to the Father but it was personal – 'Jesus is *my* way'.

> *"I am the way and the truth and the life. No one comes to the Father except through me."* (John 14:6)

For many people, this is a shocking statement. They cannot believe that a man, born in an obscure village in the Middle East over two thousand years ago, who died a miserable death, left no writings, and gave only one instruction to his followers, could be the only way to a relationship with a creator God for all peoples who in the past, and in the future will make up the world's population.

Others think that as there are many religions in the world that for the central figure of one religion to make such a claim is unacceptable and a measure of superiority that borders on hubris. Many people regard Christianity as just another religion and they rationalise the differences between religions by subscribing to the idea that all systems of religion are simply different ways to engage with a universal higher power and in the end it will all come out in the wash.

For some, it is just an impossible fairy tale, and they might as well get what they can from their earthly life by indulging in as much and as many pleasures as possible. But, as we see in Ecclesiastes, God has set eternity in the human heart and, as a result, mankind instinctively knows that there is more to life than we can fathom out on our own.

> *"I have seen the burden God has laid on the human race.*
> *He has made everything beautiful in its time. He has also*
> *set eternity in the human heart; yet no one can fathom*
> *what God has done from beginning to end."* (Ecclesiastes
> 3:10-11)

So, others believe that if there may be a higher power, they can appeal to that higher power by creating their own way. If there is a higher being, it is the 'right thing' to engage in good works and that it could be to their advantage to 'do good': generous philanthropy; community works; serving in public office; being a first responder;

serving people through medicine; becoming an elite athlete; living so as to be remembered at your funeral as 'a really good person'.

But, in the end, all of these are man-made ways to answer the nagging question: 'what is the purpose of life?'. And Proverbs warns of the result that will come about if we depend on our own ideas and perceptions: creating our own ways will have a bad outcome.

> *"There is a way that appears to be right, but in the end it leads to death."* (Proverbs 14:12)

Yes, mankind devises many 'ways', and we have considered some above, but they all have one end – death and alienation from God.

Only one way leads to life and a relationship with God the Father - Jesus!

But another meaning for the word 'way' is 'a course or route for reaching a place'. So, just as I choose Jesus to be my way to the Father and eternal life, there is a way that I need to follow by listening and obeying what Jesus tells me.

> *"This is what the Lord says—your Redeemer, the Holy One of Israel: 'I am the Lord your God, who teaches you what is best for you, who directs you in the way you should go'".* (Isaiah 48:17)

And God's direction to Peter, James, and John, when they were on the mountain with Jesus, was clear.

> *"Then a cloud appeared and covered them, and a voice came from the cloud: 'This is my Son, whom I love. Listen to him!'"* (Mark 9:7)

Throughout the Bible God is quite specific regarding 'his way'. In the books making up the Old Testament, God demonstrates his character and attributes and makes very clear to the Israelites what his way is. And Jesus reaffirms God's way.

> *"Do not think that I have come to abolish the Law or the Prophets; I have not come to abolish them but to fulfill them. For truly I tell you, until heaven and earth disappear, not the smallest letter, not the least stroke of a pen, will by any means disappear from the Law until everything is accomplished. Therefore anyone who sets aside one of the least of these commands and teaches others accordingly will be called least in the kingdom of heaven, but whoever practices and teaches these commands will be called great in the kingdom of heaven. For I tell you that unless your righteousness surpasses that of the Pharisees and the teachers of the law, you will certainly not enter the kingdom of heaven."* (Matthew 5:17-20)

Apart from this specific confirmation, throughout the Gospels Jesus, by his words and actions, clearly replicates God's character and the way God expects people to obey him (see 'My Life'). In other words, the Bible in its entirety always points us to God's way, but it is in the wisdom books (Job, Psalms, Proverbs, Ecclesiastes, and Song of Songs) that we are given a super-charged overlay of godly wisdom that will help us as we strive to follow Jesus and his example.

Jesus was always big on hyperbola, sometimes applying excessive examples (hand or eye as in Matthew 5:27-30), at other times very small examples (the mustard seed or the yeast as in Matthew 13:31-34).In a small section of the Sermon on the Mount (Matthew 7:13-

14), he tells his listeners that the gate to the life he offers is small, and the road we must follow is narrow. On the other hand, the wide gate and broad road leads to only one destination – death.

But, small or narrow, there is much we can be confident about. We are being led along this road by our shepherd, whose every care is our wellbeing. And he has travelled this road before; he knows the way and has experienced the pitfalls. He will ensure that he will care for us and will not let us slip or fall.

And, as we walk along this road, and as we read this reflection, we will be doing so in the company of hundreds of thousands of other brothers and sisters across the globe. And there are millions of brothers and sisters who have gone ahead of us, many of whom have reached the end of the road. So, as you can see, we will have many companions on the road with us, but above all, we have the friend above all others who is always with us.

Sometimes we may wonder what is coming up along the way because of our own actions or the actions of others. But we have a prophet who has told us what to expect. At times we may stumble badly, and we feel that we have lost our connection with our heavenly Father, but we have a priest with us on the road who will speak up for us and mediate for us.

Our journey will be filled with hope and joy because we know we are heading to a destination where our shepherd is the King. And we know that our King is the Lord of Lords, the creator of the rolling spheres, God the Father Almighty. All these blessings of the narrow road should encourage us to live a life of hope and joy in a way that brings the life and light of Jesus to others.

What a road! What a way! Is there any other way to live that offers such blessings and such a glorious outcome at the end?

MEDITATION – MY WAY

- Read (not sing!) through the words of the following hymn. Identify how the writer captures the truths of the gospel.

- You probably have friends or family members who exhibit the thoughts expressed in the opening to this reflection. How do you lovingly manage your relationship with them?

- What evidence is there that gives you confidence that Jesus is the only way to have a relationship with God?

- Is the 'small gate and narrow road' a difficult way to follow in this life? What external forces push against it?

- Bible reading is a great way to understand God's good and perfect way. The more we read his word the closer we draw to him. Do you set aside time to get to know God through his word?

- Do you spend time in the wisdom books absorbing God's ways? Read a Psalm or a chapter from Proverbs now. Meditate.

- Use the link or code to listen to the choir sing the hymn and thank God that Jesus is your way.

https://open.spotify.com/track/2mMe3OeOUu2eXwyXFjTRpl?si=373f3b36e6a04807

THOU ART THE WAY

Thou art the way; by thee alone
from sin and death we flee;
and they who would the Father seek
must seek him, Lord, by thee.

Thou art the truth: thy word alone
true wisdom can impart;
thou only can inform the mind
and purify the heart.

Thou art the life: the rending tomb
proclaims thy conquering arm;
and those who put their trust in thee
nor death nor hell can harm.

Thou art the way, the truth, the life:
grant us that way to know,
that truth to keep, that life to win,
whose joys eternal flow.

George Washington Doane

My End

'Glorious Things Of You Are Spoken'

In the previous reflection I said Jesus is my way, my way to the Father and eternal life. What will the end of that journey look like? I do know that Jesus will be my end and the King of the Father's kingdom. In the meantime, there are some things about my end that God has told us in his word.

Everything will be new:

> *"See, I will create new heavens and a new earth. The former things will not be remembered, nor will they come to mind. But be glad and rejoice forever in what I will create, for I will create Jerusalem to be a delight and its people a joy."* (Isaiah 65:17-18)

It will be very good:

> *"The wall was made of jasper, and the city of pure gold, as pure as glass. The foundations of the city walls were decorated with every kind of precious stone. The first foundation was jasper, the second sapphire, the third*

agate, the fourth emerald, the fifth onyx, the sixth ruby, the seventh chrysolite, the eighth beryl, the ninth topaz, the tenth turquoise, the eleventh jacinth, and the twelfth amethyst. The twelve gates were twelve pearls, each gate made of a single pearl. The great street of the city was of gold, as pure as transparent glass." (Revelation 21:18-21)

It will surpass all we can imagine:

"However, as it is written: "What no eye has seen, what no ear has heard, and what no human mind has conceived"— the things God has prepared for those who love him— these are the things God has revealed to us by his Spirit." (1 Corinthians 2:9-10)

There will be a lot of people:

"He took him outside and said, 'Look up at the sky and count the stars—if indeed you can count them.' Then he said to him, 'So shall your offspring be' Abram believed the Lord, and he credited it to him as righteousness." (Genesis 15:5-6)

We will have real bodies:

"I know that my redeemer lives, and that in the end he will stand on the earth. And after my skin has been destroyed, yet in my flesh I will see God; I myself will see him with my own eyes—I, and not another. How my heart yearns within me!" (Job 19:25-27)

There will be singing:

> *"And I saw what looked like a sea of glass glowing with fire and, standing beside the sea, those who had been victorious over the beast and its image and over the number of its name. They held harps given them by God and sang the song of God's servant Moses and of the Lamb:*
>
> *"Great and marvelous are your deeds, Lord God Almighty. Just and true are your ways, King of the nations."* (Revelation 15:2-3)

There will be praising:

> *"All the angels were standing around the throne and around the elders and the four living creatures. They fell down on their faces before the throne and worshiped God, saying: "Amen! Praise and glory and wisdom and thanks and honor and power and strength be to our God for ever and ever. Amen!"* (Revelation 7:11-12)

Nature and man will be at peace:

> *"The wolf will live with the lamb, the leopard will lie down with the goat, the calf and the lion and the yearling together; and a little child will lead them. The cow will feed with the bear, their young will lie down together, and the lion will eat straw like the ox. The infant will play near the cobra's den, and the young child will put its hand into the viper's nest. They will neither harm nor destroy on all my holy mountain, for the earth will be*

filled with the knowledge of the Lord as the waters cover the sea." (Isaiah 11:6-9)

The light will look different:

"I did not see a temple in the city, because the Lord God Almighty and the Lamb are its temple. The city does not need the sun or the moon to shine on it, for the glory of God gives it light, and the Lamb is its lamp. The nations will walk by its light, and the kings of the earth will bring their splendor into it." (Revelation 21:22-24)

There may be some surprises:

"At that time the disciples came to Jesus and asked, "Who, then, is the greatest in the kingdom of heaven?" He called a little child to him, and placed the child among them. And he said: "Truly I tell you, unless you change and become like little children, you will never enter the kingdom of heaven. Therefore, whoever takes the lowly position of this child is the greatest in the kingdom of heaven. And whoever welcomes one such child in my name welcomes me." (Matthew 18:1-5)

"But he answered one of them, 'I am not being unfair to you, friend. Didn't you agree to work for a denarius? Take your pay and go. I want to give the one who was hired last the same as I gave you. Don't I have the right to do what I want with my own money? Or are you envious because I am generous?' "So the last will be first, and the first will be last." (Matthew 20:13-16)

Relationships will be different:

> *"Jesus replied, "The people of this age marry and are given in marriage. But those who are considered worthy of taking part in the age to come and in the resurrection from the dead will neither marry nor be given in marriage, and they can no longer die; for they are like the angels. They are God's children, since they are children of the resurrection."* (Luke 20:34-36)

The tree of life will reappear:

> *"Then the angel showed me the river of the water of life, as clear as crystal, flowing from the throne of God and of the Lamb down the middle of the great street of the city. On each side of the river stood the tree of life, bearing twelve crops of fruit, yielding its fruit every month. And the leaves of the tree are for the healing of the nations."* (Revelation 22:1-2)

God will walk among us as at creation:

> *"And I heard a loud voice from the throne saying, "Look! God's dwelling place is now among the people, and he will dwell with them. They will be his people, and God himself will be with them and be their God. 'He will wipe every tear from their eyes. There will be no more death' or mourning or crying or pain, for the old order of things has passed away."* (Revelation 21:3-4)

Jesus' glory will be revealed:

"Father, I want those you have given me to be with me where I am, and to see my glory, the glory you have given me because you loved me before the creation of the world." (John 17:24)

Jesus will be 'my end':

"Look, I am coming soon! My reward is with me, and I will give to each person according to what they have done. I am the Alpha and the Omega, the First and the Last, the Beginning and the End." (Revelation 22:12-13)

MEDITATION – MY END

- Read (not sing!) through the words of the following hymn. Identify how the writer captures the truths of the gospel.

- This section gives us a glimpse of heaven. Are there any other biblical descriptions of heaven you can think of?

- Many people, including believers, have romantic, secular ideas of what heaven will be like. What do you think?

- Do the glimpses of heaven given excite and appeal to you? Why?

- The apostle Paul said he would rather be with the risen Lord than on earth (2 Corinthians 5:1-10). Do you feel that way?

- Given the riches we are promised in heaven, do you fear death, or are you excited at the idea of Jesus being your end?

- Use the link or code to listen to the choir sing the hymn and thank God that Jesus is your end.

https://open.spotify.com/track/7Ad2qekQQNPLxoKVpBiePk?si=f4e2acabe5114d9a

GLORIOUS THINGS OF YOU ARE SPOKEN

Glorious things of you are spoken,
Zion, city of our God:
he whose word cannot be broken
formed you for his own abode.
On the Rock of Ages founded,
what can shake your sure repose?
With salvation's walls surrounded,
you may smile at all your foes.

See the streams of living waters,
springing from eternal love,
well supply your son and daughters
and all fear of want remove:
who can faint while such a river
ever flows their thirst to assuage-
grace, which like the Lord the giver
never fails from age to age.

Blest inhabitants of Zion,
washed in their Redeemer's blood:
Jesus, whom their souls rely on,
makes them kings and priests to God.
For his love his people raises
over self to reign as kings,
and as priests, his solemn praises
each for a thank-offering brings.

Saviour, since of Zion's city
I, through grace, a member am,
let the world deride or pity,
I will glory in your name:
fading are the worldlings' pleasures
all their boasted pomp and show;
solid joys and lasting treasures
none but Zion's children know.

John Newton

Playlist

HOW SWEET THE NAME OF JESUS SOUNDS
The Scottish Festival Singers

THE KING OF LOVE MY SHEPHERD IS
The Scottish Festival Singers

BREATHE ON ME, BREATH OF GOD
The Scottish Festival Singers

WHAT A FRIEND WE HAVE IN JESUS
The Scottish Festival Singers

GUIDE ME O THOU GREAT REDEEMER
The Scottish Festival Singers

JESUS THE VERY THOUGHT OF THEE
The Scottish Festival Singers

BEHOLD THE LAMB OF GOD
Toronto Mendelssohn Choir

O WORSHIP THE KING
Choir of St Mary's Cathedral, Edinburgh

ALL HAIL THE POWER OF JESUS' NAME
The Scottish Festival Singers

JESUS BIDS US SHINE
Cedarmont Kids

THOU ART THE WAY, BY THEE ALONE
The Choir of Wakefield Cathedral

GLORIOUS THINGS OF THEE ARE SPOKEN
The Scottish Festival Singers

www.ingramcontent.com/pod-product-compliance
Lightning Source LLC
LaVergne TN
LVHW021615080426
835510LV00019B/2589